Seasons of the Soul

A Compilations of Poems

Valerie Champion

Copyright © 2023 by Valerie Champion

All rights reserved. No part of this book may be reproduced or used in any manner without written permission of the copyright owner except for the use of quotations in a book review. For more information, address: iam.valeriechampion@gmail.com

First Edition: September 2023

Book cover design by Badrudeen Mikaheel

ISBN <979-8-9862144-2-9>

www.iamvaleriechampion.com

Dedication

This book is dedicated to all inspiring authors, poets, and writers. We hope to inspire you to follow your writer's heart and just write! Even if you must collaborate with other writers. WRITE!!

Table of Contents

- Introduction
- Seasons of the Soul
- Seasons Change
- Sec. I - Winter's Soul
- There Comes a Time
- I AM GOD IN ACTION
- The Memory of Hands
- I'm Tired
- Sec. II - Spring's Soul
- Soul of Spring
- Something New
- Experience
- Let it Melt!
- Season of Healing
- Sec. III - Summer's Soul
- Quick Questions
- Why You Still Mad?
- Wind and Spirit
- Speak
- Sec. IV - Autumn's Soul
- Soul of Autumn
- A Little Sound
- Reflections
- My Worth
- It's a Spiritual Thing
- Sec. V - Season of Wisdom
- Season of Stillness
- Words of Wisdom
- Prayer
- What Season Could You Be Experiencing?
- Meet the Authors
- Meet the Authors
- About the Author

Introduction

We go through all four seasons here in Georgia. And in life, we will live through the different seasons at different times. Seasons of the Soul is collections of poems written by various writers. These poems represent life during each season. The book also offers wisdoms from some very wise and gracious individuals. As authors and writers, we hope you are inspired and encouraged by our written art.

Seasons of the Soul is a different kind of compilation. We hope you enjoy the variety!

Be blessed and be a blessing!

Seasons of the Soul

The seasons of the soul
Are not like the seasons of the year.
They don't come and go
In a set pattern or rhyme.

The seasons of the soul
Are more like the seasons of the heart
They come and go
As we change and grow over time.

For with every passing season,
We have a chance at a transformed life,
Becoming more of who
We are truly meant to be.

Letting go of the fleshly desires
that so bounds and hinders us.
Understanding the connection
Of the soul and spirit; that we're to be holy.

As we go through the cycle of each season
The soul goes through these changes.
And comes out stronger
And more beautiful.

For each season of the soul
Is a journey.
And each journey
Is a chance to grow
And change
And become more spiritual.

Written by
Valerie Champion

Seasons Change

Seasons change and so should we;
Striving always to grow and evolve spiritually.

Winter might be long, harsh, and cold;
It's also a time for introspection and reflection of old.

Spring is a time for beginnings anew;
When life and hope is bursting through.

Summer is passionate and vibrant;
When we feel alive, free, and filled with excitement.

Autumn is a time of harvest, and some say reaping;
When we can perhaps do a little recordkeeping.

And through it all, the old and the new,
Our spirits remain strong, unchanging, and true.

Written by
Valerie Champion

"While the earth remains, Seedtime and harvest, Cold and heat, Winter and summer, And day and night Shall not cease." - Genesis 8:22 NKJV

Sec. I - Winter's Soul

The world is hushed, in peaceful gray,
As frosty tendrils cling and sway.
The chill is sharp, but hearts are warm,
As love and hope outlast the storm.

Valerie Champion

There Comes a Time

There comes a time
When
You have to focus
Separate
When you feel hopeless
Separate from beginning to end
Let me tell you how your soul wins
It wins
It won
You did what had to be done
You cried. You lived.
You did the hardest thing
Forgive.
You forgave
You have changed
Tell me
What did you gain?
Did you gain respect or response
Did you ever decide in life
What do you want?
Did you want to make a difference?
I'm listening
I see a hint of happiness
You glistening
Did you catch it
Or let it pass
Did you see a future that would last
Or did you hold on
For too long
That's not a good trait
Or did you somehow

Start losing faith
Was that the case
I guess
The question is
Did you give it your best
Did you crack under stress
Did you ignore
The core
Of your problems
Or did you pray for God to solve them.
Did you look back
Did you get on track
Or kept running
But running where
Did you ever feel like no one cared
Or did you toss those thoughts in the back of your head
Did you give positive energy and vibes instead
Tell me what's the odds
Of you loving yourself harder
Or better
How are you improving or getting yourself together
With the weather
It changes
Get better by the day
That's ironic
How it matches your faith
You get a taste of his goodness and his mercy
He is worthy
So tell me, how
Tell me now
I need you I believe
With you
I can achieve
I just want to be amazing

I knew I was
While you were creating
Creating a masterpiece
A piece of art I am the bark on a tree I'm still standing
How can that be
Try and you will say
Read the word
I promise you
You will be heard
Speak life
Speak Christ
Speak covering
On your sister and your brother
On one another
Listen now or you'll never understand
When you feel you can't
Know you always can
Things can turn around
That's the plan
He is the God of a second chance
That's amazing
That he thought I was worth saving.
Clap clap!
Praise praise!
I will love you for the rest of my days

_____

Written by
Concetta Hardnett

I AM GOD IN ACTION

I AM the Beauty of GOD…
and ALL of His Expressions;
even the bumps and the bruises
and all of Life's Lessons.

I AM the Healing of GOD…
like the "balm in Gilead";
and the oil of Joy
whenever, I AM sad.

I AM the Happiness of GOD…
in the midst of sorrow;
singing out His Praises –
for a better – tomorrow!

I AM the Love of GOD…
from the Source of His Light;
through His Spirit, His Wisdom,
His Strength and His Might.

I AM the Power of GOD…
supplied by The Vine;
altogether Human – and yet,
Completely Divine!

I AM the Wealth of GOD…
In *The Promised Land*;
His Milk, His Honey –
and even, His "Right Hand!"

I AM the Infinite Expression

of all that I Claim – because,
I AM that I AM
is more than His Name.

I AM His Ears, His Heart –
I AM EVERYTHING, that...He Can See;
I AM that I AM
for I AM – is...
ME!!

_____

Written by
Dwayne B. Neal

The Memory of Hands

The whole house exhaled
and, as between breaths
suspending time,
the mourners shuffled bravely
in and out,
each carrying his share
of the blame, her portion
of the loss.

Some said some few words
to my Mother newly widowed.
Some could barely breathe
for the grip of grief.
If there was music,
it was sound in a vacuum.
There were flowers.
Were there colors?

Dad had died three days before
right there on the polished floor
never took another breath
I saw it all from the hallway door.

It was then a firewall fell away
sensation of blood draining,
paralysis, a psychic fracture,
a rupture not of skin but of spirit.
Did I step back,
as my body froze in place?

Did my spirit

back up a pace?

Children in the floating sea
of this dissociation drown
drifting like fragile snowflakes down
each waving
a darkened umbilical
like a salute
to truant desire
this ebbing, whispering world
singed by an unseen fire.

Seas recede, uprooted trees,
Skies collapse in fear,
Science is justly muted
before the chemistry
of a single tear.

At the smoky nub of an endless day,
remorse piled up like stones;
the graveside prayers,
the burial at the mausoleum,
I could not have guessed
what burden the unforgiven bear
or how across the fault line of years
we trace first threads of nascent grace
in wordless wounds and youthful tears.

Yet, for some things,
there's no repair
fissures of the heart
no art can bear.
No turning back.
No going on.

We are broken,
made new haunted,
like lost limbs
the memory of hands.

———————————

Written by
Russell McGuire

I'm Tired

I'm tired of wearing a mask.
I'm tired of pretending.
Masking the pain that has built up inside.
Pretending I'm alright, that things are good, all the while.

I'm tired of hiding behind a mask.
I'm tired of pretending to be an actor.
Hiding the hurt I feel from the death of my mother.
Acting like I'm not affected not knowing my father.

I'm tired of wearing this mask.
I'm tired of the game of pretending.
Masking really good my state of depression.
Pretending I'm going somewhere else yet headed to my next session.

I'm tired of covering up.
I'm tired of impersonating.
Covering up the shame from past mistakes.
Impersonating the flow of a river,
when actuality I'm a lake.

I'm tired of wearing this freaking mask.
In tired y'all, tired of pretending.
Faking the pain of abandonment and rejection.
Pretending I don't need love and affection.

I'm tired y'all, can someone help me remove this mask?
I'm tired, is that too much to ask?

_____

Written by
Valerie Champion

Sec. II - Spring's Soul

The soul of spring, so pure and bright,
Brings life anew with each day's light.
Birds sing and flowers bloom for all to see,
A season of hope, life full of possibilities.

Valerie Champion

Soul of Spring

The wind in springtime sings and hums,
Through trees and flowers, it gently strums.
It carries scents of blooming plants,
And rustle leaves as it gently chants.

It whispers secrets in your ear,
As it dances through the atmosphere.
It brings new life and hope to all,
As it answers springtime's call.

So let the wind embrace your soul,
And let its song make you whole.
For in the springtime, wind, and earth,
Combine to bring us joy and mirth.

The gentle breeze of spring,
Brings new life to everything.
Leaves rustle, flowers sway,
As the wind blows them away.

The air is sweet and fresh,
As the wind carries nature's caress.
Birds chirp and bees buzz,
As the wind blows away winter's fuzz.

The wind is a powerful force,
But in spring, it takes a different course.
It brings change and renewal,
As nature comes alive, beautiful, and true.

_____

Written by
Valerie Champion

Something New

The seasons of the soul are never-ending,
They come and go as the wind blows.
Each one bringing something new.

The winter is a time of introspection,
When we're forced to stay indoors.
And reflect on who we are
And what we want to be.

The spring is a time of rebirth.
When the frozen ground begins to thaw
And the flowers start to bloom
And we can finally see.

The summer is a time of growth.
When we're surrounded by life
And we can feel the sun on our skin
And the warmth of sunny days.

The autumn is a time of change.
When the leaves begin to fall
And the days get shorter
And we're reminded that nothing the same stays.

The seasons of the soul
come and go as we do.
Each one bringing with it
something new.

_____

Written by
Valerie Champion

Experience

Experience is the best teacher
Experience is the best feature
You could have it all
Without the
Experience
You may fall
It's your call
To learn
If you yearn
To be the best
You got to figure out a way to pass the test
Pass the test
Keep succeeding
You can do it
Keep on achieving
Give yourself a reason
To keep grinding
Continued blessings you'll keep on finding

Experience turns into chapters
That you keep running after
Experience turns into chapters
That you keep running after

I'm learning
To give All that I got
Even if that means a lot
Giving more of myself
And less to everyone else
I'm learning through experience
That things will happen

And it won't always be to your satisfaction
Don't start lacking
Find your potential
Be an impact Influential
Keep winning!
You couldn't help your beginning
But you are in control of your end
You can do all things through him, my friend
Trust and believe
That all you want to do in life you can succeed

Experience turns into chapters
That you keep running after
Experience turns into chapters
That you keep running after
Experience is the key
For you to get where you want to be!!

Experience turns into chapters
That you keep running after
Experience turns into chapters
That you keep running after.

_____

Written by
Concetta Hardnett

Let it Melt!

Let my mind dissolve in the Lord!
As I meditate on His laws.
Let it melt away like salt in water.

I want my heart to dissolve in the Lord!
As I seek to love as He loves.
Let it melt away like salt in water.

Let my soul dissolve in the Lord!
As I strive to live a holy life.
Let it melt away like salt in water.

I want my will to dissolve in the Lord!
As I surrender to His will.
Let it melt away like salt in water!

Let my whole-being dissolve in the Lord.
Let it melt away like salt in water.
Let it dissolve! Let it melt away!

_____

Written by
Valerie Champion

Season of Healing

Healing from abuse can be tough,
But you're tougher than you know.
You've got the strength to rise above,
My dear sister and let your spirit glow.

The scars that once defined your past,
Will slowly fade away.
With faith and love as your guide,
Your future is brighter each passing day.

So, hold your head high, my friend,
Walk with pride and grace.
For you are strong, you are enough,
And yes, you will find your place.

No longer held back by the pain,
You'll soar to new heights untold.
And though the journey may be long,
Your spirit will never fold.

_____

Written by
Valerie Champion

Sec. III - Summer's Soul

The soul of summer sings a song,
Of lazy days and nights so long,
Of golden rays and endless fun,
Of memories made under the sun.

Valerie Champion

Quick Questions

What if everybody, wore a disguise?
From the weak, to the noble, the simple, and the wise...
What if everybody wore a disguise?

What if everybody, donned a veil?
From the meek, to the mild, the happy, and the well...
What if everybody donned a veil?!

What if the people you hate – you were actually, meant to Love?
[and] Why is Heaven, only placed Above?!
"Heaven on Earth" – Why is this, so hard?!
WHAT IF EVERYBODY, WAS DISGUISED AS GOD?!!

Then would you Love your Neighbor – as Yourself?
and treat Everyone alike – the same, as Everybody else...
Would we still have judgments, or boundaries, or jealousy for no reason...
or lying, or stealing, or every sort of treason?!

One last question – I just gotta ask...
What if, it's – GOD (and not us) –
Who's wearing the Mask?!!

_____

Written by
Dwayne B. Neal

Why You Still Mad?

Years ago, he broke your heart.
Both of y'all moved on with a fresh start.

So, why you still mad?
Did the pain hurt that bad?

You pretended to be happy inside,
knowing full well only to yourself you lied.

Masking it was all that you knew,
because that was the easiest thing to do.

Why are you still mad?
One would think you'd be glad!

Years of secrecy was exposed,
Though there are some things left untold.

You think about it from time to time.
But thank God you found out early he was a slime.

Again, why you still mad?
One day he'll realize what he had!

_____

Written by
Valerie Champion

Wind and Spirit

As the Spirit Wind touches my face,
All I remember is His grace.
The rustling of the leaves from the trees,
The freshness of the air,
And still, all I see is His face.

Every morning His birds sing me a song.
"Chirp, chirp, chirp!
Spirit whispers in my ear,
"My grace will never steer you wrong."

Wind blows through my hair,
That's how I know You're always there.
The wind on my face,
The breeze through my hair
It's the moment I know that You are there.

Wind and Spirit,
Spirit and Wind,
This is where my life truly begins.
Wind and Spirit,
Spirit and Wind,
You're always with us,
Even to the bitter ends.

———————————

Written by
Tyra Callender

Speak

Your tongue can give life or
it can bring death.
During times of sickness,
it can bring you back to health.

Speak it!
Speak Life into those dry bones.
To all diseases or pain
say bye-bye be gone.

When God decided to create
the world we see.
He didn't use his muscles or construction workers,
He simply said, "Let there be".

Speak it!
Speak to the storms that may arise.
Speak life into your heart's desires.

Whatever you speak of can be yours.
I'm telling you the truth.
So speak it!
Speak open to those closed doors.

God said ask and you shall receive
but in your heart you must first believe!

I can only stand here and for myself speak.
Through His power, God gave me a sneak peek.

The world you have dreamed I believe you can see.
Just remember how God created the world
by simply saying let there be!

Speak it!
Speak that dream into existence.
You have the power within my friend!
Speaking it out of your mouth is simply how you begin.

Speak!!

_____

Written by
Valerie Champion

Sec. IV - Autumn's Soul

Leaves fall gently to the ground,
Colors fading, a peaceful sound.
Cool breeze whispers through the trees,
A forerunner of winter's freeze.
Soul of autumn, bittersweet,
A time of change, a time to greet.

Valerie Champion

Soul of Autumn

The soul of autumn is alive,
As leaves turn to gold and red.
Nature's beauty, a vibrant hive,
Before winter's icy bed.

Leaves rustle, twirl, and sway,
As the wind dances through the trees.
A symphony of colors on display,
The soul of an autumn day we can see.

Golden hues and fiery reds,
Mingle with shades of orange and brown.
A canvas painted by nature's threads,
As the leaves gently fall to the ground.

Cool breezes bring a crisp embrace,
And harvest bounty fills the land.
The soul of autumn, a time and place,
To pause and take in all at hand.

While the crisp air whispers a tale,
Of seasons changing and time passing by.
But the soul of an autumn day prevails,
A beauty that never seems to die.

So let us cherish this season's soul,
And savor its fleeting grace.
For soon enough, winter takes its toll,
So, autumn's beauty we must embrace.

_____

Written by
Valerie Champion

A Little Sound

The things you say to me
when I'm feeling depressed and lonely,
helps to ease my mind
and keeps me from going back in time.

A time when I was in a dark place,
walking around starving my soul
with a smile on my face.
A smile that only covered up my tears;
Tears that cried out softly to appear.

You see, closed and cold was my heart;
in my life I didn't want anyone to be a part.
I share with no one the things of my life,
until you came along shinning in your light.

Those were the days when I held everything inside,
hoping no one know or else I'd run and hide.
Then this smile of mine would turn upside down
barreling into a frown.

Then I heard the whisper of a little sound, your voice,
Saying, "My daughter to live is your choice.
You already have what it takes to win,
All you have to do is look within.

These were words no one had ever said to me,
So from my heart I thank You graciously.
Through your word you have helped turn my life around,
And it all started when I heard that little sound.

_____

Written by
Valerie Champion

Reflections

(more Quick Questions)

You think, it's hard for you...what about them??!
Your Cup runneth over:
Theirs barely reach the brim.

You feel, like it's hard for You? [just] Take a look around;
Do you see poverty growing – and, homelessness abound?
Our Lord Jesus, had no place to lay his head;
Even as a baby –*The Manger*– had no bed!

You believe, it's hard for You?
Have you considered...GOD?!!
Who sees "His" Children every day – having no regard;
For Life, for Purpose, for Holiness, not even for Direction;
Wandering aimlessly – without Guidance or Protection.

You Believe, it's hard...yeah, that might be true;
But, YOU...Believe it's hard, well, because...
it's only hard... for YOU!!
Why not, take care of others – and Let God – take care of You?
After all, ain't that what – we're supposed to do?
To bear another's burden – 'til it becomes light;
and so, we fulfill – the Law of Christ(?)!!

But...
Alas!

What we Think, Feel and Believe – will always be "The Seer";
Because we ONLY See, Ourselves...
When we look, in..."The Mirror"!!

_____
Written by
Dwayne B. Neal

My Worth

It was the same scene
Everyday
Waking up to the same four walls
Where there were no pictures on
Display

My mind kept replaying the events of
Yesterday
Thinking, how on earth
Did I allow him to decrease my
Worth
The screaming
The yelling
The calling out of
Names
Left me with feelings of guilt and
Shame

Emotions running through my
Head
And I literally just got out of
Bed
This is not how I want my day to
Start
Time to give to God the matters of my
Heart

But why am I even feeling this
Way
Come to think of it, when was the last time
I knelt to Pray

_____

Written by
Valerie Champion

It's a Spiritual Thing

It's a spiritual thing,
A force beyond our knowing.
A divine energy that sings,
In the depths of our being, glowing.

It's a connection to God of the universe,
To all that is and ever will be.
A sense of purpose and worth,
That fills our hearts with glee.

It's a journey of the spirit and soul,
A path to enlightenment and peace.
A way for us to feel whole,
And from our troubles release.

It's a spiritual thing,
A gift that we all possess.
A chance to spread our wings,
And live a life that's truly blessed.

_____

Written by
Valerie Champion

Sec. V - Season of Wisdom

A wise word here,
An encouraging phrase there,
In life's journey we go,
With wisdom to spare.
As Autumn leaves fall,
Wisdom fills the air,
As Nature's cycle completes,
We come to a time of reflection and care.

Valerie Champion

Season of Stillness

As a child, it was difficult to sit still for long periods of time. I recall memories of being told to sit still, while my mother waited to be seen by the doctor. There were magazines on the corner table of the waiting room. I would read through the pages quickly because there weren't many interesting topics. There weren't many fun things to do or play with in the doctor's office. I remember how many times I asked if we were there yet? The drive to visit family felt like hours, and it was difficult to remain still. Fast forward to adulthood and I continued to struggle with sitting still. In moments of stillness, I would subconsciously find something to do. Feeling a need to put my hands to something, instead of embracing the gift of stillness.

Seasons of stillness bring clarity and direction for the road ahead. It opens the door for quality time with the Lord. Seasons of stillness give awareness to the areas in our lives left unhealed. There will come a time in our spiritual walk in which we will have a season of stillness. This is time to reflect, prepare, confront, and plan for the assignment on our life. Seasons of stillness reveal the motives and intentions behind our actions. It uncovers the impurities and cleanses the chambers of our hearts. The seasons of stillness reveal the sovereignty and holiness of our God. I learned his voice and attributes in seasons of stillness. As it is written in the book of Psalms 46:10, *"He says, be still, and know that I am God; I will be exalted among the nations, I will be exalted in the earth."* (NIV). By the power of the Holy Spirit, we have the courage to stand and strength to be still. In seasons of stillness, we learn our God is faithful to forgive and mighty to save.

Written by Latoya Washington
Rhema Creationz
Link up with Latoya: www.rhemacreationz.com

Words of Wisdom

As a seed buried in the dirt springs upward toward the bright sun weathered by rain, out of the dirt it grows, stem by stem, leaf by leaf, petal by petal with bright colors in its complete form it turns into a beautiful flower.

This is the testimony of each of our lives how we grow through life. The light of God's grace and mercy through His son full of love knows our very purpose. We have come out of situations and storms, but they all work out for our good. We grow into a beautiful purposeful life through Christ.

Pauline Arrington
Encore Connections Group LLC

"Your gift is one "yes" away, just remember that your faith activates your true power in God that could never be cliché."

Do not fall in love with the pipe, God needs us to drink the water!

Terryn Horton-Morton
Author/Writer
Follow Anneka on IG: www.instagram.com/mygodlyspark

--

"You may doubt yourself because of your lack of education or lack of experience. But if God has called you, you aren't really doubting yourself - you're doubting the Most High. God doesn't call the qualified. God qualifies the called."

Anneka Maquay
The Collab Lift
Follow Anneka on IG: www.instagram.com/getliftedhere

--

Prayer

Father God, El Elohim, You created the seasons from the very beginning. The change of seasons has always been a part of Your purpose and promise. We know when seasons in our own lives come and go, they come to change us and help us grow. Holy Spirit, help us to experience each season with wisdom and grace. Help us to also recognize which season of life we are walking in. You tell us in Your word, "To everything there is a season, A time for every purpose under heaven". Don't let us miss the benefits of each season. When in a season of rest, may we rest. Or when in a season of harvest, may we not haste to do so.

Lord God, may we receive everything each season has to offer knowing that it is all working for our good and for Your glory. Thank You for the beauty of the seasons. Thank You, that we can witness and experience them both in nature and in our own lives. All glory, honor, and praise to You. In Jesus name. Amen.

Author of Prayer
Valerie Champion

What Season Could You Be Experiencing?

Take some time to think about the last 5 years, 3 years, year or even 6 months. Which season do you see yourself in at this very moment? Why?

_____

_____

_____

_____

_____

_____

_____

_____

_____

_____

_____

_____

Date: _____

Meet the Authors

Meet Dwayne

Dwayne Neal, is a Christian, plus an avid Student of both the Zohar and the Holy Bible. He is also the author of several books, including the God inspired: **The Greatest Affirmation in The World** (The only Law of Attraction Book, you'll Ever Need). Mr. Neal conducts several workshops and seminars in Atlanta, Georgia – where he currently resides with his family.

Link up: www.theGreatestAffirmation.com

Meet Tyra

Growing up in Alabama, Tyra began playing the flute in elementary school. During these same years, the shy 5th grader began taking the stage in musicals and singing in her local church youth choir. In high school she sang in theater musicals such as "Carnival", and "Bye Bye Birdie". Over time she began doing background vocal work for other artists, gaining experience in the music industry, developing her writing skills and confidence in her own vocal gifts. In 2005 she wrote her 1st album, "His Glory", released on Ruff Pro Records under the guidance of master guitar player and producer Keithen Ruff.

Singing and writing music made the transition to writing poetry an easy fit for Tyra. Using the imagery and descriptive play on words is similar in the craft of songwriting. All the journals and composition books that have been filled over the years have come in handy, as many of her writings and inspiration comes from the many pages that are full of ink and her tears. "Writing has always been a big part of my life. Even as a young girl, I would have writing competitions with my BFFs, copying pages and pages of books. Didn't know at the time that God was preparing me to be a writer. But not just poetry, but also music and as an author of my own books.

Tyra is a daughter, a sister, aunt, and grandmother. She spends her days playing with her grandbabies, writing, and doing service work in local and national community groups. Recently she has answered the call to the ministry. "My greatest love is my Lord and Savior Jesus Christ, who has given me a new life and 2nd, 3rd, 4th chances again and again. I am nothing and can do nothing without Him. It's because of Him that I can do all of these things. To Him be the glory"

Meet Russ

Russell Rutland McGuire Jr. was born in Washington, DC in 1949. Like so many of that generation I wasted my time tipsy on double malt whiskey, idling over the poetry of Robert Bly, which, as I recall, was populated with impotent lumberjacks in those days before the four-hour erection. We had fun and didn't look too far ahead.

I grew up in a world of one-legged men, so full of subtext and back-story, you'd think, from their silence; they were anything but the glorious conquerors of boundless evil. As their son, I listened for some word from them. Spent entire summers on the beach by the canasta tables, filling their glasses and carrying out the trash, driven only to see fulfilled that look I took for longing. But there would be nothing again in this world to charm them. Eyes turned inward as if to distant beaches and the sound of cannon fire. And so, I listened to echoes. Seas in shells. Whispers so hoarse with their own truth as to speak with the broken voices of the dead, to whom, I was convinced they too listened.

I learned to listen for it. Between the lines of idle chatter and endless card games until, nothing having passed their lips but prayer, I learned what they could not tell me and never would. That time folds origami-like upon itself, doing its best to cloak our secrets in silence. And that, it is left for us, who follow, to listen and to learn.

I'm in my 74th year. Like many of my generation, I never thought I'd live this long. I'm a poet and father of three daughters. I hope to leave them more than hurt and sorrow suffered in silence.

I'm still fishing with baited lines. Always on the run. Too clever for my own good. Tomorrow is stressed to the breaking. I am reconciled to this ground-hog town, ripe with funky onions. And only now am I able to forgive those who came before and left too soon.
I'm ready to put down my crazy broken world at the doorsteps of overrated Angels on a casting call with God. I am prepared to do hand-to-hand combat with the coming of the 360-degrees of silence.

Meet Concetta

Concetta Hardnett is a 35-year-old Laureate poet, writer, and songwriter. I reside in the Atlanta Metro area. Poetry use to be a hobby for me but after writing for so many years, it's me, it's my life, it's what I love to do.

Just knowing that my words have inspired and helped so many people, most importantly, I've helped myself. My writings, when I look back, give me hope and gave others hope. I'm so grateful that I was blessed to be the voice behind the pen.

Meet the Authors

Meet Latoya

Latoya Washington is the wife of David Washington, business owner of RhemaCreationz, host of *"Broken Vessels Podcast"* and Author of *"Broken Vessels: Letters to Abba"* & *"Concrete Rose: Secrete place in Abba"*. She furthered her education by attending Cheyney University but obtained a Bachelor of Science Degree at Elizabethtown College. She continued her education by attending Liberty University in Lynchburg, Virginia and received a Master of Arts Degree in Human Services with a focus in Criminal Justice. Her passion for writing created an opportunity to be featured in two anthologies, "We all belong" and "Ruth &; Naomi Experience". Her literary work has been featured in several online magazine platforms which include, "Growth Women's Business Network Magazine, RGP Music Publishing, Heart of Flesh Journal, and SpeakUpSis magazine. She continues to live by the motto, "it is possible to love again, live again and laugh again"!

Meet Pauline

Pauline Arrington is music lover and a lover of Christ Jesus. She is also the owner of **Encore Connections Group LLC**; where she offers consulting services in fashion, entertainment, marketing, and public relations.

Link up:www.encoreconnectionsgroup.com

Meet Terryn

Terryn Yancey Morton, a Christian author, blogger, poet, Wife and Mom, who loves God with all her heart. I am imperfect yet still able to see so much beauty in the world. My love for Faith & Fairytales inspired my book titled "*Their Innocence, My Hustle, Our Growth: A Modern Faitherella Story*"! Here is a little advice, and I am still learning things for myself, God created each of us with unique talents. We shine brighter because we all have something different to bring to the masterpiece which is God's creation. We are meant to be more than servants to our personality flaws that try to hinder us from our growth in God.

Link up with Terryn: oursparkblog.com

Meet Anneka

Anneka Maquay, an Entrepreneur and owner of **The Lift Collaborative Group**. She is a Kansas City native, who now resides in Georgia. Anneka is also the Co-founder of Show Me Shoes, a 501(c)(3) non-profit organization whose vision is to create a movement.

Link up with Anneka: instagram.com/getliftedhere

Website: https://showmeshoes.org/
Contact: info@showmeshoes.org
www.facebook.com/ShowMeShoes

About the Author

Valerie Champion is founder of Transforming Prayers Ministry, a prayer ministry. She is author of the self-published books titled "Expressions of the Soul, Volume I & II", both are a collection of poems; "It's a Spiritual Thing, a prayer manual and journal, My 52 Weeks Affirmation Journal and several other books and journals. As an entrepreneur in her own rights, Valerie is a Certified Christian Life Coach and Prayer Counselor. She is the founder of Transforming Prayers podcast and Your Spiritual Tea blog on YouTube. Valerie is also the proud owner of Champion Travel Escapes travel agency. Your one-stop-shop for all your travel needs.

Valerie is an advocate for abused women and has tailored her coaching program around helping the abused to heal past their pain. She obtained a BA in Marketing from AIU in 2006 and graduated Cuma Sum Laude; all the while working a full-time job at one of four P.R.O.'s in the country. She is passionate about her spiritual life. Her belief is that we are all here to help one another navigate through life. She believes we all have a story to share that will help inspire, encourage, and heal others.

Valerie was born and raised in Atlanta Georgia, where she graduated from Booker T. Washington High School in 1987. Though she only has two sons, she's known as mother of many. The love of her life is her grandson, Braylen. She now resides in Douglasville Georgia, where she is a dedicated member of Let's Live Christian Family Fellowship Church.

www.ingramcontent.com/pod-product-compliance
Lightning Source LLC
Chambersburg PA
CBHW050919160426
43194CB00011B/2472